For Jack,
Best Wishes for Christmas
and the New Year.
Ron
December 1981

The First Sunrise

AUSTRALIAN ABORIGINAL MYTHS

THE
FIRST SUNRISE

AUSTRALIAN ABORIGINAL MYTHS

IN PAINTINGS BY **AINSLIE ROBERTS**

WITH TEXT BY **CHARLES P.MOUNTFORD**

Line Illustrations by Ainslie Roberts

RIGBY

The Dreamtime Series
By Ainslie Roberts and Charles P. Mountford
The Dreamtime
The Dawn of Time
The First Sunrise
The Dreamtime Book
By Ainslie Roberts and Melva Jean Roberts
Dreamtime Heritage

RIGBY PUBLISHERS LIMITED • ADELAIDE
SYDNEY • MELBOURNE • BRISBANE
NEW YORK • LONDON
First published 1971
Reprinted December 1972
Reprinted February 1974
Reprinted August 1974
Reprinted January 1978
Reprinted May 1979
Reprinted November 1980
Copyright © 1971 Ainslie Roberts and Charles P. Mountford
ISBN 0 85179 253 7
All rights reserved
Typeset and designed in Australia
Printed in Hong Kong

TO THE BROWN PEOPLE
who handed down these Dreamtime Myths

CONTENTS

THE
FIRST SUNRISE

The profound mystery of the creation of the Universe has occupied the beliefs of people from the simplest cultures to those of the present day. Almost without exception, except perhaps in some aspects of modern life, these beliefs have played a major part in moulding the philosophies and even the way of life of the people to whom they belong.

The myths of the Australian aborigines, which deal with the creation of their Universe and the establishment of the rules of human behaviour that all must follow, are accepted as revelations of absolute truth and are the foundations of their social and secular and ceremonial life. The re-enactment of these beliefs in the ceremonial grounds provides the actors with a deep religious experience, comparable to that of a practising Catholic taking part in the Mass.

These myths also describe how, before creation times, the uncreated and eternal earth had always existed as a large flat disc floating in space. Its uninhabited surface was a vast featureless plain, extending unbroken to the horizon. No hills or watercourses broke its monotonous surface, no trees or grass covered its nakedness, nor did the calls of birds or animals disturb its quiet. It was a dead, silent world. Yet, slumbering beneath that monotonous surface, were indeterminate forms of life that would eventually transform the forbidding landscape into the world as the aborigines know it today.

As the ages passed, these mythical beings began to emerge from beneath the plain and to wander haphazardly over its surface. These newly-created beings seem to have resembled creatures or plants in appearance, but to have behaved like human beings. They camped, made fire, dug for water, performed ceremonies, and fought each other, because there were good and evil people in those early times just as there are today. The aborigines do not believe in a Golden Age in which all was perfect.

Then, suddenly, creation time came to an end. The mythical creatures died, but each place in which one or another of them had carried out any task or feat, or had acted in some significant or memorable way, is now marked by a natural feature.

When they were asked what had brought about this remarkable change, the aborigines admitted that they did not know, although they had often discussed the matter among themselves. But, they said, some of the wise old men of the past could have answered the question. They themselves could not explain the great change in which the world passed from mythical times, when the world was being created, to secular or historical time, when the creation of the world was complete.

Since the aborigines look upon themselves as the direct descendants of one or another of those mythical beings of the past and each, in turn, lives in the country created by them, it follows that every man, woman, and child is linked intimately, both by myth and lineage, with everything in the aboriginal environment. This is a very close personal link that dominates all aspects of their life, both sacred and secular.

Any white man who has travelled alone with a group of aboriginal men, in places far removed from the haunts of other white intruders, will have soon become aware of the close personal links between these people and their country and the affection which they feel toward it. Everything that they see about them is reminiscent of their creation and proof of the authenticity of the ancient stories; the hills, the rocks, the conformation of the land, the waterholes, the trees, and even, in some places, the grass between the trees.

Their fundamental belief is that all secular activities, all the patterns of the tribal ceremonies, and all the laws that govern both secular and ceremonial behaviour were decreed by the mythical creators of the long-distant past.

The aborigines live in a realm of unchanging behaviour, extending from mythical times, through the present and on to the distant future. To the aborigines, there never has been, nor will there ever be any change in their lives. What happened in the past is happening now, and will go on unchanged forever.

The myths that support these philosophies provide the aborigines with a reasonable explanation of the world in which they live; the stars above them, the natural forces of wind, rain, and thunder and the plants and creatures that provide them with food.

Over most of Australia, the sun is looked upon as a woman, who rises every morning, to provide light and heat for the world. At the end of the day she travels through a long underground route to reach her camp in the east, to begin yet another journey across the sky. The moon is looked upon as a man, who makes the same journey at different times from the sun, but dies for three days every month and is eternally restored to life.

The myths concerning the constellations of Orion and the Seven Sisters, although widespread through the continent, vary considerably. In the southern parts of Australia, the Seven Sisters are said to be the wives or daughters of Orion, who go over the horizon some time before the men in order to make their camps and cook the food.

In the desert country, however, the relationship between Orion and the Seven Sisters is always one of conflict. The women forever flee from one place to another to escape his unwelcome attentions. The route travelled by this mythical group extends for long distances across central Australia.

The Milky Way is looked upon as the "River of the Sky" from which, when the sun sets, the sky people catch their food; stingrays, turtles and fish. Some tribes consider that the myriads of stars in this heavenly spectacle are the camp-fires of the celestial people.

In Arnhem Land, great mythical snakes travel from place to place in the thunderclouds of the wet season. Their spears are the lightning, and their voices are the thunder. In some places these snakes also send the tiny child spirits down in the rain drops so that they can become human babies.

On Groote Eylandt, the Magellan clouds are the camps of an old man and a woman, who are always being looked after by the other inhabitants of the sky. On the other hand, the aborigines of central Australia believe the inhabitants of the same constellations to be unfriendly toward the people on earth, and that they will sometimes do them harm.

A study of aboriginal astronomy has also revealed that the natives have developed a well-defined calendar, on which they base their food-gathering journeys, totemic rituals, and seasonal movements.

In many parts of Australia, a number of spirit people live in the surrounding country. Though the local aborigines have never seen them, their dwelling places and characteristics are well-known and they have often been heard scrambling amongst the rocks at night.

These spirits are of two kinds; the Mamandis, malicious ill-disposed demons who are always on the lookout to injure or destroy the aborigines; and the Mimis, shy, harmless little sprites who are of no danger to anyone.

The Mamandis are much feared, although there is little danger from being attacked if two or more aborigines travel together. There are also the giant rainbow serpents of the rivers and deep waterholes, who will drown anyone foolish enough to drink their water without taking the necessary precautions; the Namarakains, who are forever trying to steal the spirits of sick people from their bodies; and the Nabudi women, who maliciously use barbed darts from their own bodies with which to kill aborigines.

The myths of the major creators, whose paths of travel often pass through many tribal areas, fulfil the most important function in tribal life. These myths explain the origin of every topographical feature, great and small; the creation of life in its many forms; the origin of the natural forces; the weapons to be used by hunters; and, most important of all, they decree the rules of behaviour that all must obey to ensure the harmonious functioning of their society.

The myths are of two general forms: those which tend to concentrate around some important natural feature or totemic place, and others, known as the travelling myths, that describe the travels of important creators as they moved across the country.

The most detailed study yet made of aboriginal beliefs belonging to a unit of topography is that associated with Ayers Rock (Uluru), the enormous isolated monolith which rises eleven hundred feet above the level deserts of central Australia. During creation times, Ayers Rock was a level sandhill; the home of a number of mythical beings, birds, animals, and reptiles. At the close of the creation period, when Ayers Rock assumed its present form, the marks of the activities of the people were changed into the natural features and markings on the monolith; the high vertical cliffs; the deep gutters on its vertical faces; the water-holes at its base, and even the water-stains and patches of lichen on its sides. These topographical features and markings are, to the aborigines, visual evidence of the activities of their mythical creators.

However, the myths associated with localities such as Ayers Rock are not so important to the aborigines as the travelling myths that describe how the creators of the long-distant past travelled across the country, often for hundreds of miles, creating all the natural features along the route, bringing into existence the topography, the animals, and the food plants, and at the same time decreeing the procedures of the rituals that admit men to a higher social status.

A number of mythical creators along the eastern coasts of the continent, such as Baiami and Daralulun, made their home in the sky when their work on the earth was completed. But Nurunderi, the creator of the River Murray and the lakes at its mouth, and Witana, an important creator of the northern Flinders Ranges of South Australia, were both transformed into parts of the landscape. On the northern coasts many of the important creators were women, such as the Djunkgao and Wawalik sisters of Arnhem Land and the Minyaburu women of north-western Australia. But in the desert country of central Australia it was a kangaroo, Malu; a euro, Kunjula; and the fairy owl, Tjulki, which carried out the same duties and decreed laws similar to those elsewhere in the continent.

One myth of the desert people relates how a woman, Kutunga, gave birth to children who were later miraculously transformed into egg-shaped boulders on the open plain. It is believed that these boulders are filled with an inexhaustible supply of spirit-children, the Yulanya.

The aborigines, who were not aware of the facts of physical paternity before the arrival of the white man, believed that their spirit children, who originate in many different places, were self-existent little beings who first chose their own mothers, then entered their bodies to begin life as human beings.

From the beginning of their lives, aboriginal children grow up in a secure atmosphere of affection. The little fellows are looked after and caressed by everyone with whom they are in contact, and are not secluded from the life around them. As they grow older, and are no longer dependent on their mothers, they join other children of their own age; playing in the sands of the creek bed, or sitting around their tiny fires chanting their childish songs. Except for the hardship that Nature inflicts on these little people during the long desert journeys, it would be difficult to imagine a more ideal life for the development of any child.

But not many years elapse before the division of the sexes takes place. The boys go out in groups to capture, cook and eat the smaller wild life, while the girls accompany the women on food-gathering journeys to learn the techniques of gathering and winnowing grass-seeds and digging out underground foods and small hidden creatures. From then onwards, the life of the girls changes little until their marriage, when they set up camps of their own and acquire the additional duties of wives and mothers.

The development of the life of the boys follows an entirely different pattern. As they grow older they spend most of their time with the men; sitting around their camp fires, listening to their tales of hunting and travel, or accompanying them on short hunting journeys. But the boys are not, as yet, allowed to take part in the hunts for the larger creatures. In their ignorance of hunting skills they might alarm the prey, or the journeys might be too strenuous for them. When the huntsmen set off on such journeys the boys either hunt by themselves, following the tracks of the lizards and such small creatures; or constructing "hides" beside small rock-holes in order to spear the small birds as they come in to drink; or they play their spear games on the open plain.

When the facial hairs of the youth begin to grow, he knows that he is approaching the important period of his life; that of initiation. Although this rite varies widely throughout Australia, they all involve the initiate in a long series of sometimes painful rituals, and a complete obedience to the old men during his long journey to tribal manhood.

The rituals in which he takes part will teach him, by strange ceremonies and long tiring journeys, the rules of behaviour laid down at the beginning of time and the penalties of non-observance. Later, in an aura of mystery, the initiate will have to endure ordeals of pain and trials of fortitude that will impress his receptive mind so deeply that their meanings will never be forgotten.

At the conclusion of these rituals, which extend over several years, the newly initiated man can marry and may sit in the tribal council, although his opinions will not yet carry much authority.

But, as he grows older, his tribal status will increase with his knowledge of the secret life of the tribe, until the old men will at last consider that he has sufficient knowledge to be admitted to their exclusive circle.

The aborigines do not understand death from natural causes. They believe that it is the result of the ruthless magic of some enemy, and many are the strange and complex rituals performed to identify the murderer. Once this has been established a party will leave to avenge the death. They make a great show of violence, but as the identity of the supposed murderer is usually not well defined, or, more often than not, he belongs to a different tribe, the members of the avenging party are usually back in camp next morning, and everyone is satisfied.

Almost all methods of disposal of the dead are practised by Australian aborigines; burial in deep graves, exposure on a platform, smoke drying, and even cremation. The final home of the spirit of the dead also varies widely. Some tribes believe that the spirits return to the boulders from which they originated; others that they go back to their mythical tribal country, and follow a way of life similar to that which they knew on earth; others again that they travel to distant islands where conditions of living are ideal. And, in some tribes, the spirit simply ceases to exist. The use of his name is forbidden and all memory of him disappears.

CHARLES P. MOUNTFORD

St. Peters, South Australia

ALINDA THE MOON-MAN

Many aboriginal myths explain how death first came to the world but only two, this one from Arnhem Land and that of Purukupali's Whirlpool, from Melville Island, describe how the moon-man partly escapes this decree. The myth says that, during creation times, the parrot-fish man Dirima and the moon-man Alinda constantly disagreed over trivial matters. During one particularly violent quarrel, the two men inflicted such terrible wounds on each other that they both died. The spirit of Alinda then transformed himself into the moon and rose into the sky; while Dirima became the parrot-fish which now lives in the sea.

But the moon-man continued the quarrel, and decreed that when the time came for the parrot-fish to die he, as well as all other living things, would never return to life. The moon had to obey his own decree, but partially escapes it by dying for only three days, then coming to life again and resuming his journey across the sky. The aborigines believe that the skeleton of each dead moon drops into the sea and becomes the empty shell of the chambered nautilus.

The aborigines also have an explanation of the relationship between the tides and the moon. When the tides are high the water, at sunrise and sunset, runs into and fills the moon. As the tides become progressively lower, the water runs out until, for three days, the moon is empty. Once more the tides rise, the moon fills, and the everlasting cycle repeats itself.

The Bones of the Moon

27″ x 36″   *Mr and Mrs B. J. Scanlen*   17

THE NIGHT HERONS
AND THE REEDS

In northern New South Wales there was once a small tribe of aborigines who were so badly treated by their neighbours that for protection they changed themselves into herons, made their home in a swamp, and hunted only at night.

Although it was seldom that anyone interfered with them in their new home, the herons did not feel safe. The swamp had little cover because in those days the reeds were only thin short grasses, insufficient to conceal the movements of the birds.

The herons overcame this problem by stretching the stems of the plants, and as time went on these short grasses developed into reeds that were higher than the birds.

But even now, the herons do not feel entirely secure. Although the high reeds conceal their movements, these birds hunt only in darkness, and never leave the shelter of their swamp.

And to prove the truth of this myth, aborigines point to the nodes on the reed stems. They say that these are the places where the herons gripped the reeds with their beaks, to make them grow taller.

27″ x 36″   *Mrs M. J. Roberts*   19

WIRANA'S CAVE

There are many tall, grotesque human figures painted in the caves of the rugged Kimberley Ranges of north-western Australia. According to native beliefs, these paintings are not the work of the aborigines, but of the Wandjina people who lived in that country during the time of creation. All Wandjina paintings are associated with some particular creature or plant.

At the close of the creation period, each Wandjina painted his own likeness on the wall of a cave, then entered either the rock-face on which he had painted his image, or the water of a nearby spring. At the same time the spirits of the Wandjinas decreed that, with the beginning of every wet season, each painting should be renovated by its associated aborigines. These renovations cause the spirit to impregnate its own special creature or plant, and thus provide an abundance of those foods.

The painting on the facing page is based on a myth associated with the eagle-hawk, Wirana, who built herself a nest on the top of a tree, laid two eggs, and started to incubate them. But one day, while she was absent, Wandjuk the rock-pigeon stole the eggs and hid them.

When Wirana returned and found what had happened, she swooped down to destroy the thief. But Jundum the owl, a friend of the pigeon, threw a boomerang at Wirana and killed her.

As she was dying, Wirana transformed herself into a Wandjina painting on the back wall of a cave, while her two eggs were changed into boulders at its mouth. Now the men of the eagle-hawk totem renovate this painting at the beginning of each wet season, so that its spirit will increase the number of young eagle-hawks.

27" x 36"   *Private Collection*   21

GARKAIN THE RECLUSE

The aborigines of Arnhem Land people their country with a host of spirit beings. They still live in the deep caves and high crevices of the eroded plateau, among the rushes and water-lilies of the swamps, and under the tall trees of the stringy-bark forests.

The most feared of these beings are the Namarakains and the Nabudi women. The Namarakains are always trying to steal the spirits of sick people; while the dreaded Nabudi women, from sheer malice, project invisible barbs into the bodies of solitary men who travel by themselves, and make them sick.

But there are others who are generally less dangerous, though they may become violent if anyone trespasses in an area which they regard as their special domain. Among their number is a dumb spirit-man, Garkain. His home is in the dense jungle along the banks of the Liverpool River. Should anyone venture into that jungle Garkain, who can fly as well as walk, will wrap himself around the intruder, and smother him with the loose folds of skin which are attached to his arms and legs. As Garkain has neither tools nor weapons, he has to catch what living creatures he can with his bare hands. He does not know the secret of fire, so he has to eat them raw.

However, most of the spirit-beings of Arnhem Land are harmless, and never molest the aboriginal people.

36″ x 27″   *Mr and Mrs Charles O'Connor*   23

HERITAGE OF THE
BLACK SWANS

In the days of the Dreamtime all swans were white. During that time, two swans rested on a lagoon, unaware that it belonged to the eagle-hawks. The eagle-hawks resented this intrusion, and savagely attacked the swans. Then they picked them up in their sharp, strong claws, and flew with them far to the south. Even while the swans were being carried away to this strange new land other eagle-hawks tore at their wounded bodies, plucking out still more feathers. Finally, the swans were dropped on the rocks of a stony desert.

There, naked and almost dead, the swans heard the call of the black mountain-crows. They looked up and saw hundreds of them; either on the wing or struggling for places on the few branches of the desert trees. "The eagles are our enemies too," the crows called out, in their strange, croaking voices. "But we won't let you die. We will send down on the breeze some of our feathers to keep you warm, and when you feel strong enough they will help you to fly again." The torn-out white feathers of the wounded swans, taking root between the rocks on which they fell, grew into the dainty flannel flowers of the eastern Australian coast, and the blood of the birds was transformed into the blossoms of the scarlet heath. And ever since that day all Australian swans, except for a few white feathers on their wings, have feathers as black as the crows which clad their nakedness and helped them to fly again.

Heritage of the Black Swans

Ainslie Roberts
1966

27″ x 36″   *Mrs B. L. Brennan*

25

THE SOUND OF THUNDER

The aborigines of Melville Island believe that their universe is divided into four levels. These are the underground world, Ilara; the earth on which they live; the sky-world, Yuwuku; and an upper world, Tuniruna.

Yuwuku, the sky-world, is the place of the stars and moon at night, and the sun-woman Wiriupranali by day. In Ilara, where it is always dark, the sun-woman, after her daily journey across the sky, makes her nightly return trip from west to east, guided only by the light of her smouldering fire-stick. The moon-man, Japara, goes the same way, but his time of travel varies.

Tuniruna, the upper world, is the daytime home of the sky-people. During the dry season it is also the home of Pakadringa, the man of the thunderstorms; Tomituka, the woman of the monsoon rains; and Bumerali, the lightning-woman. Quork-quork, who is the tree-frog nowadays, was at the time of creation the mother of Pakadringa, Tomituka, and Bumerali. It was said that, should any aboriginal injure or ill-treat this frog, her children would revenge her by causing so much rain that everyone would be drowned.

Pakadringa, Tomituka, and Bumerali always travel together. At the end of the dry season they leave the upper world, Tuniruna, and move from place to place in the sky-world, shedding rain on the parched earth beneath. Bumerali the lightning-woman carries in each hand a stone axe with which she strikes the ground, destroying the trees and everything else in her way. Her voice is the sharp crack of thunder that immediately follows the lightning flash. The first sound of thunder is welcomed by the male initiate in the Kulama ceremonies, for it is his signal that he may at last discard the elaborate designs painted on his body. But he is the exception; to all other aborigines thunder is the sound of terror, for many of them have been killed with the stone axes of Bumerali.

"The First Sound of Thunder"   Ainslie Roberts
                                                                              1968

27" x 36"   *Mr James S. Anderson*   27

THE ANT-HILL MAN

The aborigines of the high plateau country of western Arnhem Land believe that many spirit people live in the country round about them. Some of these are harmless, and some dangerous to human beings.

Although the aborigines know the characteristics and the dwelling places of each of the spirit people, they have never seen them. But they claim that the medicine-men of the past, being much cleverer than those of the present generation, had the power to see these mysterious beings.

Buma-Buma, one of these harmless spirit people, lives by himself in one of the huge termite mounds that abound in that area. Buma-Buma dislikes walking any distance and although he owns a spear, a spear-thrower, and a knowledge of fire-making, his food consists almost entirely of honey from the hives of the wild bees in the termite mounds, and the flesh of the small creatures, such as bandicoots, lizards and echidnas, which live in the ant-hill country.

27″ x 36″ *Mrs M. J. Roberts*

29

WURIUPRANILI
THE SUN-WOMAN

One of the astronomical myths from northern Australia describes how the sun-woman, Wuriupranili, and the moon-man, Japara, travel at different times across the sky. Each carries a torch of flaming bark, but when they reach the western horizon they extinguish the flames and use the smouldering ends to light their way as they return eastwards through the darkness of the underground world.

Each morning, the fire lit by the sun-woman to prepare her torch of bark provides the first light of dawn. The clouds of sunrise are reddened by the dust from the powdered ochre which she uses to decorate her body. It is then that the soft, melodious call of Tukumbini, the honey-eater, wakens the aborigines to the duties of another day.

At sunset, Wuriupranili reaches the western horizon. But, before she returns by an underground passage to her camp in the east, she again decorates herself with red ochre, thus causing the brilliant colours of sunset.

Waller and the Red Ochre.   Ainslie Roberts
1970

36″ x 27″   *Mr and Mrs Malcolm E. Gaetjens*

THE EMU AND THE TURKEY

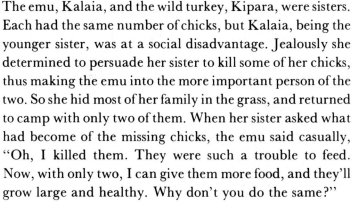

The emu, Kalaia, and the wild turkey, Kipara, were sisters. Each had the same number of chicks, but Kalaia, being the younger sister, was at a social disadvantage. Jealously she determined to persuade her sister to kill some of her chicks, thus making the emu into the more important person of the two. So she hid most of her family in the grass, and returned to camp with only two of them. When her sister asked what had become of the missing chicks, the emu said casually, "Oh, I killed them. They were such a trouble to feed. Now, with only two, I can give them more food, and they'll grow large and healthy. Why don't you do the same?"

Naturally the wild turkey did not like the suggestion, but it sounded reasonable. So she took her chicks into the bush and killed all but two, but was furious, on her return, to find that she had been tricked, and that Kalaia still had her original family.

She planned revenge, and a few days later she folded her wings so tightly against her body that they seemed to have been cut off. Dancing in front of her sister, the wild turkey explained that she had found her wings far too heavy. "Besides," she said, "I'm sure I look more beautiful. Why don't you do the same?"

The emu, foolish as well as jealous, was too vain to resist the idea, so she cut off both her wings with a stone knife. With a cry of joy the wild turkey rose into the air. "You stupid bird!" she taunted. "Now you have no wings and cannot fly, and men and dogs can run you down and kill you. But I can always escape."

This myth explains why the wild turkey, who hatches only two chicks, can fly, while the emu, with her many chicks, is always in danger of being captured by her enemies.

27″ x 36″   *Mr H. C. McDonald*   33

NURUNDERI AND THE COD

The aborigines who once lived on the shores of Lake Alexandrina, at the mouth of the River Murray, left behind a number of interesting stories about the exploits and adventures of the man Nurunderi, who created the fish in its waters and many of the natural features along its banks.

Nurunderi was a tall, powerful man, who once had a riverbank camp on the upper Murray. From this camp his wives deserted him, taking their children with them.

One day, when Nurunderi saw a huge cod swimming down stream, he followed it in his bark canoe. In those days the River Murray was only a small stream, but as the cod swam away from Nurunderi its great body burst through the land and enlarged the river to its present size.

By the time Nurunderi had followed the cod as far as Lake Alexandrina, he had almost given up hope of capturing so large a fish. Then he remembered that his brother-in-law, Nepele, lived further down the Lake, and might be able to spear it. So Nurunderi signalled Nepele that a large cod was swimming towards him, and Nepele managed to spear the fish as it passed near his camp.

The two men then created all the fish in Lake Alexandrina and the Murray by cutting the cod into many pieces which they threw into the water. As they did so, they decreed that one piece would become the perch, another the callop, another the mulloway, and so on, until all the present day fish were named. A large part of the cod still remained, so Nurunderi threw that into the water, saying, "You continue to be a Murray cod."

Having completed his task of peopling Lake Alexandrina and the river with fish, and being unable to find his wives and children, Nurunderi made his camp with Nepele on the shores of Lake Alexandrina.

Creation of the Nursery.

Ainslie Roberts
1966

27″ x 36″   *A.M.P. Society*

WYUNGARE AND THE
AVENGING FIRE

Wyungare, who lived on the shores of Lake Alexandrina, was a famous hunter, and so handsome that the two wives of Nepele fell in love with him.

They made an opportunity to visit his camp, and found him asleep. So they imitated the sound of running emus, and Wyungare awoke. He grabbed his spears and rushed to kill the birds; but instead of emus he saw the two women. They begged him to keep them in his camp; a request to which he readily agreed.

When Nepele heard what his wives had done, he was so angry that he hurried to Wyungare's camp to avenge the insult. When he found that all three had gone hunting, he punished them by laying a magic fire just outside their shelter. He commanded it to burst into flame when the culprits were asleep and, if they escaped, to follow them.

The magic fire obeyed his command, and pursued the hunter and the two women as they fled along the shores of Lake Alexandrina. At last, in desperation, they immersed themselves in the muddy water of the Lowangari swamp, and the fire drowned itself in its efforts to reach them.

Wyungare then decided that the only way to escape the hate of Nepele was to live among the stars. So he tied a rope to a barbed spear and threw it up into the sky, where it became firmly fixed. Wyungare and the two women then climbed to the stars, where they have lived ever since.

The myth also relates how Wyungare, when he lived on earth, once caught a giant kangaroo and tore it into pieces. He scattered the pieces throughout the land, and from these fragments grew all the various kinds and sizes of the kangaroo family.

42″ x 62″   *Whaler's Inn, Rosetta Bay*   37

THE BRINGER OF FIRE

In the early days of the world the only aboriginal who knew how to make fire was Mar, the cockatoo-man; and he was so selfish that he would not share his secret with anyone.

The aborigines, growing more and more angry with the cockatoo-man and more and more envious of his fire, determined to discover the secret. They sent the little bird-man, Takkanna, to find how fire was made. Takkanna waited until Mar had meat to cook, and then hid behind a low bush to watch him. He saw Mar lay dry grass and bark on the ground and place the meat on top. Mar then raised his hand to his head as if to scratch himself, but instead he took fire from under a bunch of feathers he wore as a head-dress.

When Mar was not looking, Takkanna pushed the flower stem of a grass tree into the fire. As soon as it was well alight, he, taking the burning stem in his arms, hurried back to his companions. But, as he ran, sparks fell into the grass and started a fire that spread over a huge area of the country. When Mar could see how the fire had been caused, he screamed with rage. But when he attempted to attack little Takkanna, he was stopped by the other aborigines.

During the fight, all who took part were turned into birds. The cockatoo-man, still screaming angrily, flew into a tree. The red feathers on his head still show where he had kept his fire. Takkanna was changed into a robin redbreast, its scarlet feathers being a reminder of how, unselfishly, he had given fire to his people. Since then the aborigines have always had fire; to keep them warm, to cook their food, and to dispel the darkness of night.

The Fire-Maker

Ainslie Roberts
1964

36″ x 27″   *Mr and Mrs Andrew Tennant*   39

NUNGA THE PIGEON

This myth is associated with the sea-gull man, Shivra, and the Torres Strait pigeon-man, Nunga. It explains why, at the beginning of each wet season, the pigeons leave Papua and fly to the Australian mainland. There the birds nest and rear their young, and return to their homeland when the monsoonal rains are over. The aborigines of the area claim that this annual migration originated during creation times when the pigeon-man had a large family. Two of them were beautiful girls, whom the sea-gull man, Shivra, stole and carried away in his canoe.

Nunga's family was very angry over the abduction and urged Nunga to take revenge. But as Shivra was his friend, Nunga refused to act. This decision led to so much family quarrelling that Nunga left his family in disgust, and travelled along the coast until he reached two large rocks that marked the place where Shivra had earlier wrecked his canoe. Here Nunga transformed himself into a Torres Strait pigeon and flew to Papua.

But Shivra, with the two girls, walked across the Torres Strait to Papua. Their path across those waters is now marked by the many islands which rose from the footsteps of Shivra and the girls.

27″ x 36″   *Private Collection*   41

THE FIRST RETURNING
BOOMERANG

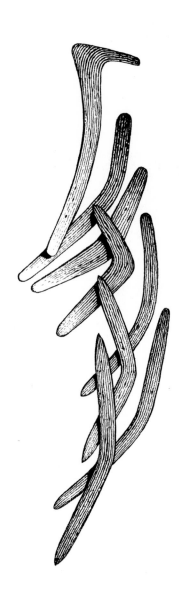

The Australian boomerang is a specialised sharp-edged throwing stick which, when thrown at considerable speed and with a vertical spin, can inflict a serious or even fatal wound. A skilful boomerang thrower is often remarkably accurate, and is able to hit and disable a kangaroo at distances of up to fifty yards. However, this weapon is only effective in comparatively open country, for low trees or high grass will divert its flight and destroy its accuracy.

Contrary to a general belief, the boomerang is not in use in all parts of Australia. It is seldom used in the central Australian deserts, because the spear and spear-thrower is a much lighter and more effective combination. Nor is it used in large areas along the northern coasts, where the country is heavily wooded.

As a weapon, the returning boomerang has many limitations. It is effective only when thrown at right-angles to the wind, and even the slightest obstruction will interfere with its spin and cause the weapon to fall harmlessly to the ground. It is likely that, before the arrival of the Europeans, this type of boomerang was restricted to the southern coasts. But the interest of the white man in the flight of this strange weapon, and the fantastic stories told of its capabilities, undoubtedly increased the area of its distribution.

The painting is based on a myth about the creation of the Flinders Ranges of South Australia, and relates how the lizard-man, Kudnu, made the first returning boomerang. When he first threw it into the air, the peculiar action of the boomerang so attracted the attention of the small mallee trees at Waraminta that, in trying to follow its curious flight, their upper branches became much twisted and distorted.

24″ x 36″   *Mrs Rhys Roberts*   43

MUDUNGKALA THE CREATOR

Before the first sunrise, all was darkness. The earth was flat and featureless. No hills or valleys broke its monotonous surface, no trees covered its nakedness, nor did the call of birds disturb its silence.

Then, during those far-off times, an old blind woman, Mudungkala, rose miraculously out of the ground, carrying in her arms three infants; a boy and two girls. No one knows whence she came nor, after she had created the land of Tiwi, where she went.

Crawling on her hands and knees, she travelled in a wide circle. The water that bubbled up in her track became the swift tideway that now separates Melville Island from the Australian mainland.

But, before Mudungkala left, she decreed that the bare land she had created should be clothed with vegetation and inhabited with creatures, so that her children, and the generations to come, should have ample shelter and food.

Kala creates the Sea.

36″ x 27″   *Mr Richard S. Cohen*

PURUKUPALI'S WHIRLPOOL

Purukupali, one of the great creators of the Tiwi tribe of Melville Island, had an infant son, Jinini, whom he loved very much. But one day Jinini died. His mother, Bima, had neglected him while she was with her lover, Japara.

On hearing of the child's death, Purukupali became so enraged that he beat his wife over the head with a throwing-stick, and hunted her into the jungle; he then attacked her lover with a club and covered his face with deep wounds.

Despite this, Japara wanted to help the anguished father to restore his son to life within three days. But Purukupali angrily refused the offer. He picked up the dead body of his son and walked into the sea, calling loudly as the waters closed over his head, "As I die, so all must die and never again come to life," a decree that brought death to all the world.

The place where Purukupali drowned himself is now a large and dangerous whirlpool in Dundas Strait, between Melville Island and the mainland. In this place the current is so swift and strong that any aboriginal attempting to cross the maelstrom in a canoe would be drowned.

When Japara saw what had happened he changed himself into the moon and rose into the sky, with his face still bearing the scars of his wounds. But, although Japara cannot entirely escape the decree of Purukupali, and has to die for three days each month, he is eternally re-incarnated.

27″ x 36″   *Mr and Mrs Roy Griffiths*   47

MILAPUKALA THE COCKATOO-WOMAN

When Jinini, the son of Purukupala, died, his father was so frenzied with grief that he drowned himself in a whirlpool off north-western Melville Island. In those remote times, when a death was to be mourned in the Pukamuni burial ceremony, it was the duty of Tukumbini the yellow-faced honeyeater to call the mythical beings together to carry out the rituals.

At the conclusion of the rites, they returned to their camps in various parts of the island to create food for the aborigines who would later populate the land.

The cockatoo-woman, Milapukala, had her camp at Cape Fourcroy, on south-eastern Bathurst Island. She made a large fresh-water lagoon, Milapuru, and then many rocky headlands and open plains around its shores. She then decreed that many food creatures should make this place their home, so that there would be much food in the country she had created.

Her duties completed, the cockatoo-woman transformed herself into a cleft rock on the shores of the Milapuru lagoon. At fixed times every year, the aborigines of that country assemble at the totemic rock and perform rituals to commemorate the exploits of Milapukala, as well as magically to increase the creatures and plants.

27″ x 36″   *Mr and Mrs B. J. Scanlen*

THE DEATH OF KULTA

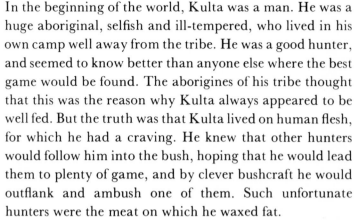

In the beginning of the world, Kulta was a man. He was a huge aboriginal, selfish and ill-tempered, who lived in his own camp well away from the tribe. He was a good hunter, and seemed to know better than anyone else where the best game would be found. The aborigines of his tribe thought that this was the reason why Kulta always appeared to be well fed. But the truth was that Kulta lived on human flesh, for which he had a craving. He knew that other hunters would follow him into the bush, hoping that he would lead them to plenty of game, and by clever bushcraft he would outflank and ambush one of them. Such unfortunate hunters were the meat on which he waxed fat.

At last, the tribe realised that the disappearance of so many of their hunters was no coincidence. They suspected Kulta, and after two more hunters had disappeared they raided his camp. To their horror, they discovered the truth.

They speared Kulta to death, and buried him in the bank of a creek near his camp. That night, the creek came down in flood, and washed the body out of the earth and into the lagoon. There, Kulta's body turned into an enormous snake, which lived in the depths of the lagoon and still possessed his craving for human flesh. In search of it, Kulta the snake travelled great distances from the lagoon by digging channels and letting the water flow along with him, because he could not live out of the water. He moved so fast that no aboriginal could escape him.

But Kulta had to die a second time. One very hot day, he went too far from the lagoon, and the water in his channel dried up before he could return. The aborigines now say that the dry channels radiating from the lagoon, which fill with water only in the wet season, are those which were dug by Kulta.

27″ x 33″   *Private Collection*

THE CROCODILE-MAN AND THE PLOVER-MAN

Another myth which describes how fire was saved for mankind belongs to western Arnhem Land.

In the days when the world was young, the crocodile-man, Gumangan, and the plover-man, Birik-birik, owned a pair of sticks which, when rubbed together, produced fire. They were the only sticks of their kind in the world. Gumangan and Birik-birik always travelled together, but Birik-birik was such a lazy fellow that the crocodile-man did most of the work.

One morning, as the crocodile-man was leaving the camp to hunt, he asked Birik-birik to light the fire so that, when he returned, they could cook the food he had caught. Hours later, when the crocodile-man came back carrying a large kangaroo, Birik-birik was asleep and there was no fire.

The crocodile-man, thoroughly annoyed with his lazy companion, lost his temper. He abused the plover-man for his laziness, snatched the fire-sticks from the ground, and ran towards the nearby river to dip the sticks into the water and so extinguish fire for all time. But Birik-birik acted quickly. He grabbed the fire-sticks from Gumangan and ran into the hills.

Since those times the crocodile has always lived in or near water, and the plover in the hills or on the open plains. Today the aborigines fear the crocodile, but look with much pleasure on the plover who saved fire for mankind.

The Lonely Crusader

Brett Roberts
1971

36″ x 27″   *Osborne Art Gallery*

53

GURUGADJI THE EMU-MAN

In the Oenpelli area of Arnhem Land there are many creation stories concerning mythical serpents. Most of these creatures, under different names, spend the dry season in deep water holes. During the period of the monsoonal rains, they live in the thunder-clouds.

The aborigines fear these mythical serpents. They believe that any interference with their waterholes would cause the serpents to destroy them, or to cause the water to overflow and flood the whole country.

This myth relates how, in the early days of the world, two aborigines were out hunting when they saw an emu, who, unknown to them, was the mythical emu-man, Gurugadji.

The hunters crept up and tried to capture Gurugadji. One of them took hold of him by the neck, and the other by the head, but he escaped them and jumped into a waterhole. There he transformed himself into the rainbow serpent, Mamaragan, emerged again, and swallowed both the hunters.

Mamaragan, like all rainbow serpents which appear in the sky in the form of the rainbow, is much feared by the aborigines. For, if he becomes annoyed, he will swallow them as he did the two hunters of so long ago.

The First Rainbow

27" x 36"   *Mr and Mrs L. M. Lee*

55

THE PARROT-FISH ROCK

This painting depicts the myth of the parrot-fish man, Yambirika, who in the long distant past made a camp on Bickerton Island in the Gulf of Carpentaria.

After living there for a while he became dissatisfied with the site. So he dug a hole through the ground (which the aborigines of that country believe is just resting on the surface of the ocean) and entered the sea. There he created two magical places where the aborigines, by performing rituals, are able to increase the number of parrot-fish.

The first of these two places, Talimba, is a loosely arranged circle of stones on the sea-shore, where the sand within the circle is heavily impregnated with the spirits of parrot-fish. At the breeding time of these fish, the aborigines take handfuls of the sand and cast it in all directions, at the same time chanting a song asking that there will be parrot-fish everywhere.

At Bartalumba, the other increase centre, the parrot-fish man has been transformed into a rock. The top projects only a few feet above the sea, and the ritual consists of breaking off small pieces of rock and throwing them in all directions, meanwhile chanting the same song as at Talimba. The aborigines believe that these rituals are always effective, and not only multiply the number of parrot and other fish in the locality but make them easier to catch on their fishing lines.

The Parrot-fish Rock

Noelle Roberts
1926

27″ x 36″   *Mrs John S. T. Cox*   57

THE KINGFISHER AND
HIS WIVES

One South Australian myth tells how the Kingfisher-man, Yulu-yuluru, was forever quarrelling with his wives, Wanatjilda and Mundikara, because he thought they did not bring him enough to eat. When Wanatjilda explained that there was little food to be gathered at that time of the year, the Kingfisher-man told her to stop talking, and walked away. This rudeness so infuriated the two women that they decided to eat everything they collected.

When, on the following evening, Yulu-yuluru asked for his meal, the women said there was none. Grumbling, the Kingfisher-man walked to his camp and was soon asleep, for already he had caught and eaten two goannas. The women told him the same story for several days, but he knew they were lying. Otherwise, they would have complained about hunger. So he decided to teach them a lesson.

Soon he saw an emu drinking at a waterhole, and signalled his wives to drive the bird towards him. Being tired of seed cakes they cheerfully did so, and the emu was speared. But when the women suggested that Yulu-yuluru should cook the emu at their fire, he told them gruffly to go back to their camp and wait until they were called. Yulu-yuluru cooked the bird, made himself a waterproof shelter, and then created such a heavy storm that its flood waters rushed down the creek and surrounded the small island on which the women were camped. Knowing they could not escape, Yulu-yuluru threw stones at his wives. He wounded them so badly that, to save their lives, Wanatjilda turned herself into a diver-duck and jumped into the flooded stream, while Mundikara, becoming a water-hen, disappeared into the reeds.

And that, so the aboriginal women tell their children, is why the diver-ducks are so clever at dodging stones, and the water-hens always hide in the reeds.

27" x 36"   *Mr Harry A. Badenoch*

WITANA AND THE OCHRES

Witana was a giant mythical being of the tribes of the northern Flinders Ranges in South Australia. He created many of the natural features of that beautiful country; its steep-sided gorges, brightly coloured cliffs, and permanent water-holes. Witana also established the rites of initiation, particularly the Wilyeru body-scarring ceremony through which all aboriginal youths must pass before they can achieve full tribal manhood.

According to the traditional stories, Witana once camped at Wataku-wadlu, in the middle of the Flinders Ranges. While he was there he made a cut in each of his arms, to obtain the blood with which to decorate youths taking part in the initiation rituals. The pool of blood which ran from one arm was transformed into a deposit of red ochre, and that from the other arm became a reef of black pigment.

In times past the local aborigines, as well as those of more distant tribes, made annual pilgrimages to Wataku-wadlu to gather these pigments for the initiation of their boys. The red ochre was used for the circumcision ceremonies, and the black pigment for the body-scarring rituals of the Wilyeru.

Vilana's Ochre Mine.

36″ x 36″   *Dr D. H. Le Messurier*

61

THE MEDICINE-MAN

The medicine-man is a person in whom the aborigines have much faith. Yet he has a family, he hunts with his companions, he takes part in the secular and ceremonial life of his tribe, and is subject both to sickness and to death. But he is a man apart, because the spirits of dead medicine-men, the Wulgis, have admitted him into their world of healing and magic; a world that few aborigines can enter.

When the Wulgis notice an aboriginal who shows more than ordinary interest in the psychic life of the tribe, they choose him to become a medicine-man.

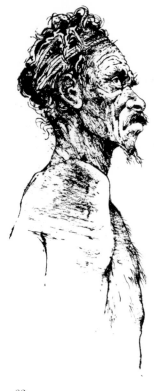

The Wulgis wait until the initiate is asleep, take the spirit from his body, and change it into the form of an eagle-hawk. Then they conduct it into the sky, where it is shown many wonders and the secrets of magic and healing which are known only to the medicine men. At dawn, the spirit of the initiate is taken back to his camp, transformed from that of an eagle-hawk to that of an aboriginal, and returned to his own body. These journeys are repeated many times before the initiate has learnt all the secrets of his profession.

On return to his ordinary life, the newly initiated medicine-man has many new powers; he can heal the sick, find the spirits of children who have lost themselves in the darkness, and hunt the malignant night spirits from the camps.

Occasionally the medicine-man will seek the help of a Wulgi spirit to cure an aboriginal suffering severe body pains. The Wulgi goes inside the patient and searches until it finds an object such as a stick or stone, which has been placed there by an enemy. The Wulgi gives this to the medicine-man, who shows it to his patient as evidence that the cause of the pain has been removed.

It is said that the patient always recovers. No aboriginal ever doubts the ability of a medicine-man to cure most forms of sickness, or to overcome the effects of evil spirits.

27″ x 33″   *Mr K. P. Mountford*

NARADAN THE BAT

When Naradan the bat-man was searching for honey he found a hive in a hollow gum-tree. So he sent one of his wives with a stone axe to cut out the hive and bring the honey back to the camp. But when the woman pushed her arm into the hole, her feet slipped, and she could not get her arm out. Naradan was more interested in the honey than in his wife, so he cut off her arm and she died.

Naradan then told his second wife to climb the tree, pull out the arm of the dead woman, and return with the honey. The woman objected to this gruesome task, but Naradan threatened her so violently that she made the attempt. But her arm, too, became jammed. Naradan, more furious than ever over the loss of the honey, climbed the tree and tried to release her arm, but killed her also.

The bat-man, now thoroughly ashamed of himself, returned to the camp. But, as he refused to answer any questions about his missing wives, their mother sent out some young men to find out what had happened. When they returned and told the gruesome story, the tribesmen were so horrified that they built a huge fire and threw the bat-man into it. As the flames rose higher and higher, and the heat became more intense, the people saw a dim figure rise out of the flames and vanish into the darkness.

Naradan, now a bat, is so ashamed of his former behaviour that, to avoid being seen, he sleeps during the day and hunts for his food only when there is no light in the sky.

27" x 36"   *Chrysler Australia Limited*   65

CRAITBUL'S OVENS

Geologists tell us that the craters at Mount Gambier are the result of volcanic activity. But, according to the ancient stories of the aborigines, it was a giant man, Craitbul, and his sons, who created these natural features.

Craitbul and his sons had only one tool, a wooden digging-stick. With this simple tool and their bare hands they dug out their daily food, the underground tubers. They cooked these in an earth oven.

This mythical group established their first camp at Mount Muirhead, where they lived happily for a long time. They spent the time in gathering and cooking their food, or just resting near the oven until the meal was ready. But one night an enemy attacked Craitbul and his sons. He frightened them so badly that they fled to Mount Gambier, where they felt sure that they would be safe.

After digging another oven, the giant and his sons again lived in peace. But one day, without any warning, water bubbled up into the bottom of the cooking oven and put out the fire. Craitbul dug another oven, but the same thing happened again, and yet again, until four ovens had to be deserted. Disgusted by their misfortunes, Craitbul and his sons departed in search of a place where they might dig another oven, but no one knows where they went.

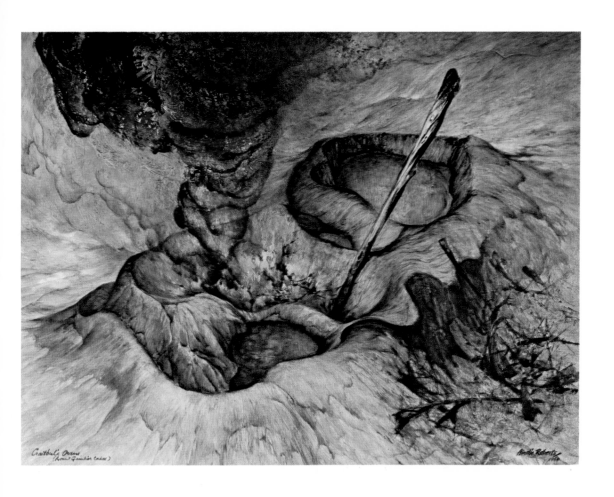

Craitbull's Ovens
(Mount Gambier caves)

Nettie Roberts
1969

THE ORIGIN OF DAY AND NIGHT

In the days when the world was young, light was provided by the great fire on which the cannibalistic sun-woman, Bila, cooked her human victims. At that time the lizard-man Kudnu, who was a famous boomerang-thrower, and the gecko-man Muda, paid a visit to their neighbours, the euro-people. They found that all the euro-people had been killed by the dogs of the sun-woman and dragged to her camp. Angered by this bloodthirsty deed, the lizard-men decided to kill Bila in revenge.

When the sun-woman saw Kudnu approaching she howled with rage. She snatched a boomerang from her belt to throw at him, but she was too slow. Before she could throw her weapon, Kudnu's boomerang had wounded her so badly that she, transforming herself into a ball of fire, disappeared over the horizon, leaving the world in complete darkness.

The lizards were terrified by the calamity they had caused, but Kudnu decided to use his remaining boomerangs to try to bring the light back again. He threw one of them to the north, but the darkness still remained; he then threw two more, one to the south and one to the west, but still there was no change. But when he threw a boomerang to the east, the lizards saw a great ball of fire rise, travel slowly across the sky, and disappear below the western horizon, thereby creating day and night.

After this, no aboriginal in the Flinders Ranges would kill a goanna or a gecko. They said that these creatures not only saved mankind from destruction, but created day and night; the day in which to gather food, and the night for rest and sleep.

Kudnu, Mirrla
and the Sun-Woman

Ailsie Robertson

27″ x 33″   *Miss A. M. Davidson*   69

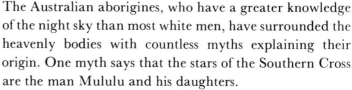

THE SOUTHERN CROSS

The Australian aborigines, who have a greater knowledge of the night sky than most white men, have surrounded the heavenly bodies with countless myths explaining their origin. One myth says that the stars of the Southern Cross are the man Mululu and his daughters.

Mululu, the leader of the Kanda tribe, had four daughters of whom he was very fond, but to his sorrow he had no son. When he grew old, he called his daughters together to discuss their future. He said that he expected to die soon, so, since they had no brother to protect them from the spite and jealousies of the women or from being forced into marriage with a man whom they disliked, he wanted them to leave the earth when he died and to meet him in the sky. The father then explained that, with the aid of spirits of the night, he had recently visited a clever medicine-man, Conduk, who was willing and able to help the girls reach their new home.

When their father died, the daughters set out to find Conduk, whose camp was far away to the north. They had to travel many days before they reached it, and they recognised Conduk by the long thick beard by which their father had described him. Resting beside his camp was a huge pile of silver-grey rope, which the medicine-man had plaited from the long hairs of his own beard. One end of the rope reached up into the sky.

The girls were terrified to learn that the rope was their only means of reaching their father again. But with the guidance and encouragement of Conduk they climbed to the top of the rope, where they were delighted to find their father waiting for them.

Now, the daughters are the four bright stars of the Southern Cross. Nearby and caring for them is their father; the bright star Centaurus.

27" x 36"   *Mr and Mrs H. A. Treloar*

THE WONGA PIGEON AND THE WHITE WARATAH

This story was told by an old aboriginal who lived in the Blue Mountains, and it explains why only an occasional white waratah may be found although such flowers are usually red.

The old man said that, long ago, all waratahs were white. In those days, the first wonga pigeon camped in the forest with her mate, and they grew fat on the rich food on the ground. They never flew above the trees, because they were afraid of their enemy, the hawk.

One day the wonga pigeon's mate went hunting for food, but did not return to their camp. She became anxious and set out to search for him, but without success.

After she had been searching for a long time, she plucked up her courage and decided to fly above the treetops in an attempt to see him from a height.

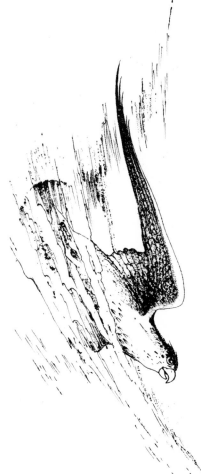

She had just left the shelter of the trees when she heard the call of her mate down in the forest. With her heart full of gladness she turned to fly down to him.

But she was too late. The circling hawk had seen her. Swooping down, he clasped her in his sharp claws, tearing her breast open as he carried her upwards. Her blood rained down on the forest, but she tore herself free and hid among the blossoms of the waratahs.

The hawk had just flown away when she again heard her mate calling to her. Although she was weak from loss of blood, and could fly only short distances, she endeavoured to reach him. Every time that she rested on a white waratah, to recover her strength, her blood stained its bloom. In a final struggle she reached yet another waratah, and there she died as the last blood ebbed from her wounded body.

Today, the old man explained, it is possible, though it is rare, to find a waratah that has not been stained by the blood of the lonely wonga pigeon who lost her life while searching for her mate.

27″ x 18″   *Dr and Mrs Graham W. Welch*   73

THE CROW-MAN WHO
STOLE FIRE

A myth from eastern Australia relates how the secret of fire
was known only to seven women, the Karak-karak, who
would not reveal how their fire was made. But the crow-
man, Wakala, determined to find out their secret. He made
friends with the women, and by accompanying them on
their food-gathering journeys he discovered that they
carried fire in the end of their digging-sticks. Also, he found
that the women were particularly fond of termites, but
were equally afraid of snakes.

So he buried a number of snakes in a termite mound, then
casually told the women that he had found a large nest of
termites. He offered to show it to them, but as soon as they
broke it open the snakes attacked them. Terrified, the
Karak-karak protected themselves by hitting the snakes
with their digging-sticks. They killed many snakes, but also
caused fire to fall out of the sticks. The crow-man quickly
picked up fire between two pieces of bark, then fled to his
camp and started a fire of his own.

The Karak-karak women, furious over losing their
exclusive ownership of fire, rose into the sky to become the
constellation of the Seven Sisters. The crow-man, now the
owner of fire, refused to share it with anyone. He simply
called out "Wah wah," in a mocking voice, whenever he
was asked. His selfishness led to so much quarrelling that
he, losing his temper, threw some coals at one of the men.
When these coals started a bushfire he rushed to his camp
for shelter, but that too caught fire and he was burnt to
death.

Yet, even as the aborigines watched, they saw the charred
corpse of Wakala come to life, change into a crow, and fly
to the upper branches of a tree, still calling out "Wah wah"
derisively.

27" x 36"   *Mrs M. J. Roberts*

BARA THE NORTH-WEST WIND

The aborigines of Groote Eylandt recognise two main winds; the north-westerly, Bara, which blows from November to March and brings the monsoons, and the south-easterly, Mamariga, whose dry season extends from April to November. The aborigines believed that during the dry season the north-westerly wind was imprisoned in a large, hollow tree at Maijunga, in the Gulf of Carpentaria.

When the wet season is approaching, the aborigines assemble around the wind tree at Maijunga, and by making deep cuts in the bark with their stone axes, they release the Bara wind. At the same time, the assembled tribesmen chant a song telling the wind to go into the sky and form cumulus (wet season) clouds. The aborigines claim that, on the morning following this ritual, the Bara wind would be blowing and the wet season clouds beginning to form.

The Groote Eylandt winds are associated with the two main social groups; the Bara to the Oranikapara, and the Mamariga to the Wirinikapara. Each group believes that their children are brought to them on these winds. For example, the Oranikapara group believe that a spirit child brought in on the Bara wind hides in the grass until it sees a woman of that group, then enters her body to be born as a human child. The Wirinikapara group have a similar belief about the Mamariga wind.

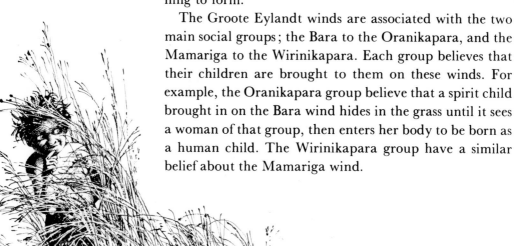

Retreat of the North West wind

27" x 36"   *Osborne Art Gallery*

77

THE WATERS OF NIRGO

A long time ago, when the two dingo-men Munbun and Kapiri were on a desert journey, they became very thirsty. So they started to dig for water at Nirgo. Munbun, the younger, spent many hours making a long burrow towards the north, but without success; Kapiri, however, working in the opposite direction, soon discovered a spring of clear water.

While the dingo-men were resting, two medicine-men came along. Naturally the dingo-men invited them to drink at the newly-dug spring, and then told them that as Nirgo was the only spring in the desert, they would give it to the aborigines. The medicine-men were very impressed by this generosity, and made a new law that, for ever afterwards, aboriginal hunters could kill only the father dingoes, and not the mothers nor the pups.

This decree was obeyed for a long while, until a selfish aboriginal killed and ate two dingo-pups. When the culprit heard the mother dingo calling for vengeance, he knew that his only chance of escaping death was to get off the ground. He climbed a tree and sat on a high branch.

But the mother persuaded other dingoes to uproot the tree. Working slowly and surely, they dug away at its roots until, with the terrified aboriginal still clinging to its branches, it fell with a mighty crash. The body of the aboriginal was broken into many pieces, but the dingo pups were miraculously restored to their mother.

There is now a large hole in the ground where the tree once stood, with many red boulders scattered around it. They represent the congealed blood of the aboriginal who so foolishly broke the law of the medicine-men.

"Dingo and the Law-breaker"

Áodío Roberts
1968

36" x 27"   *Mr James S. Anderson*